The MAILBOX®
The Education Center®

THE ULTIMATE Classroom Solutions

Early Childhood

Teacher-tested ideas for successful classroom management

- Back-to-school
- Routines and procedures
- Getting and staying organized
- Learning centers

- Student behavior and motivation
- Partnering with parents
- Documentation and assessment
- And MORE!

Managing Editor: Kelly Robertson

Editorial Team: Laura Abert, Becky S. Andrews, Diane Badden, Amy Barsanti, Amanda Boyarshinov, Janet Boyce, Amy Brinton, Kimberley Bruck, Karen A. Brudnak, Ann Bruehler, Julie Christensen, Cathy Coil, Clare Cox, Pam Crane, Chris Curry, Beth Deki, Amber Dingman, Amy Erickson, Pierce Foster, Jennifer Frankle, Irene Giannotti, Heather Graley, Colleen Gregory, Karen Guess, Tracie Hagler, Jesse Hall, Tazmen Hansen, Terry Healy, Marsha Heim, Lori Z. Henry, Tracy Hora, Shelley Hoster, Lorna Kearns, Debra Kelley, Sheryl Konopack, Kwin Kunkle, Danielle L. Lampert, Debra Liverman, Kitty Lowrance, Roxanne Ly, Naomi McCall, Beverly McCormick, Harmony Mitchener, Suzanne Moore, Tina Petersen, Gerri Primak, Kerry Prodromides, Mark Rainey, Jennifer Reidy, Greg D. Rieves, Hope Rodgers-Medina, Keely Saunders, Rebecca Saunders, Darlene Taig, Donna K. Teal, Sharon M. Tresino, Susan Walker, Laura Wanke, Carole Watkins, Zane Williard, Kate Wonders, Barbara Worobey, Virginia Zeletzki, Katie Zuehlke

www.themailbox.com

©2012 The Mailbox® Books
All rights reserved.
ISBN 978-1-61276-149-7

Except as provided for herein, no part of this publication may be reproduced or transmitted in any form or by any means, electronic or mechanical, including photocopying, recording, or storing in any information storage and retrieval system or electronic online bulletin board, without prior written permission from The Education Center, Inc. Permission is given to the original purchaser to reproduce pages for individual classroom use only and not for resale or distribution. Reproduction for an entire school or school system is prohibited. Please direct written inquiries to The Education Center, Inc., P.O. Box 9753, Greensboro, NC 27429-0753. The Education Center®, *The Mailbox*®, the mailbox/post/grass logo, and The Mailbox Book Company® are registered trademarks of The Education Center, Inc. All other brand or product names are trademarks or registered trademarks of their respective companies.

Printed in the United States
10 9 8 7 6 5 4 3 2 1

HPS 233447

Table of Contents

Student Behavior and Motivation

Partnering With Parents

Documentation and Assessment

Working With Colleagues

Personal and Professional Development

Index

FREE Online Extras!

Follow these steps to get your **FREE** online extras!

1. Go to www.themailbox.com.
2. Click on "Register."
3. Register your copy of *The Ultimate Classroom Solutions*. Your item number is 61334.

How do I **get organized over the summer**?

✱ Be sure to discard unneeded materials. For example, instead of keeping extra photocopies of handouts and practice pages, file one master copy and recycle the rest. Also, shred and discard student papers and information related to your last class. Toss any outdated decorations or materials as well. You'll have a fresh start in the fall!

Summer Projects
• Organize math manipulatives.
• Add to word wall words.
• Fix globe.

✱ Take advantage of the summer break to work on school projects that you don't have time for during other times of the year. Throughout the year, keep a list of such projects. Once school is out, you'll be ready to tackle the list!

✱ Since summer is a great planning time, why not revamp lessons that you feel need improvement? Consider changing the materials or approach you use. It's a wonderful way to re-energize your teaching!

✱ Take some time to revisit your classroom procedures. Think about the ones you currently have in place, and consider how you can increase your effectiveness and decrease students' time off task. Jot down notes about the ideas you would like to try and how you can implement them during the school year.

How do I **prepare for my first-ever class**?

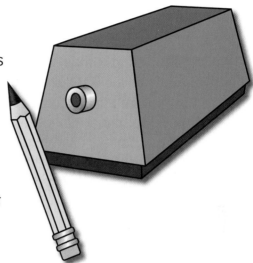

✳ Keep rules and routines top of mind. Before the school year starts, plan how to handle procedures such as students' arrival, turning in notes and other paperwork, going to the bathroom, sharpening pencils, and other reoccurring classroom routines. Then set aside time on the first day to explain the procedures to students. Follow up by demonstrating procedures and inviting students to practice them. It's bound to get the year off to a smooth start!

✳ When planning your lessons for the first week of school, plan twice as many activities as you think you will need. It is easy to underestimate how long activities will take. If you are over-prepared, it's no problem. Simply save the extra lessons and materials for another day.

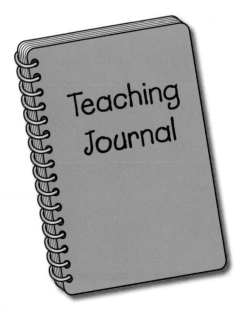

Teaching Journal

✳ Prior to the start of school, begin a teaching journal. Write in it a few goals that describe what you would like to accomplish during the school year. Then, periodically throughout the year, reflect on your teaching. Write about your successes and the areas you need to improve in order to achieve your goals.

How do I **help youngsters deal with the first-day jitters**?

✳ Bring comfort to an uneasy student on the first day of school by having him bring along a special stuffed toy to school. Whenever he needs to be soothed, allow him to cuddle his toy. The familiarity of the toy is bound to have a calming effect.

✳ Help youngsters transition into the first day of school with hands-on centers. When children arrive on the first day, have centers set up with materials and activities such as play dough, painting, and a cooking project. Keeping little ones busy helps minimize their fears and calm their nerves.

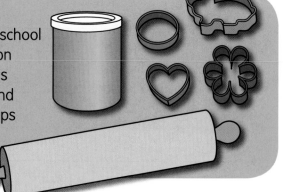

✳ Get youngsters acquainted with their classmates before school begins! Arrange a play date at a local park two to three weeks prior to the start of school. Invite each student in your class to attend. Students will get to know each other in advance and will look forward to starting school and seeing their new friends!

How do I **get to know my new students**?

✱ Since students' families know them better than anyone, who better to share student information with you? Send home a survey with students asking questions about their likes, learning habits, interests, and any other areas you'd like to learn about. Have their families fill out the surveys and return them to school. Count on families to give you great insights!

✱ For each child, label a card with her name, address, parent or guardian contact information, and dismissal information. Then attach her photo to the card. Hole-punch the cards and place them on a metal binder ring. The ready access to student information is sure to come in handy while you're getting to know students and their parents.

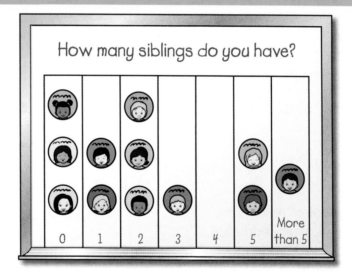

✱ Get to know your students as you help them get to know each other! Trim a head-and-shoulders photo of each student and attach it to a colorful paper circle labeled with his name. Adhere a magnet to the back of each circle. On each of several days, write a getting-acquainted question on the board; then draw and label one column for each answer choice. Read the question to students and then have each youngster move his circle into the appropriate column. Discuss the results of the graph with the group to explore similarities and differences among students.

How do I **establish class rules**?

✳ Keep classroom rules simple for little ones. Tell students that they need to take care of only three things: themselves, their classmates, and their school. Make a poster for each rule. When a student makes a poor behavior choice, point out the appropriate poster and give her a gentle reminder about how she is breaking that rule.

Take care of yourself.

Take care of your classmates.

Take care of your school.

✳ Establishing the consequence for breaking a classroom rule is almost as important as the rules themselves! After establishing class rules, identify a consequence for breaking each rule. Post the list of consequences near your rules. Students appreciate knowing what to expect.

✳ To help youngsters remember rules for different procedures, break the rules into manageable chunks. On separate sheets of tagboard, write the rules for daily occurrences such as lining up, going to the restroom, and taking naps. Post the signs near the locations where the rules will most likely be followed.

Lining Up

1. Push in your chair.

2. Keep your hands and feet to yourself.

3. Be quiet.

How do I **establish class rules**?

✱ To help students learn the right way to do things, model following the rules and breaking the rules. Students benefit from seeing the rules in action, plus they enjoy seeing their teacher "break" the rules!

✱ Here's a picture-perfect way to help youngsters quickly learn your classroom rules. Photograph students following each classroom rule. List the rules on a large poster and attach each photograph beside the corresponding rule. Display the poster in a prominent location. Even if a child is unable to read the rules, your expectations will be clear from the photos.

✱ Encourage youngsters to manage their behavior with beautiful blossoms. Write each classroom rule on a paper flower cutout. Then tape a jumbo craft stick to the back of each. Insert the sticks into a large piece of green foam. When you need to introduce a rule, pick the appropriate flower from the garden and discuss the rule.

How do I **host a successful open house**?

✳ Prior to open house, take photos of your students participating in daily classroom activities. (Be sure every child is in at least one photo.) Mount the photos on poster board and add captions. Display the photos at their corresponding centers or classroom areas. During open house, parents will enjoy seeing their children in action as they learn about the day-to-day happenings in your classroom.

✳ Invite students to give their parents a quick classroom tour! To prepare, poll students a few days before open house to determine the five most popular classroom items or areas. Prepare a numbered list of the top vote getters. Label each featured attraction in the classroom with a numbered sign and set copies of the list near the classroom door. The lists will be perfect references for your young tour guides.

✳ Challenge your open house guests to identify their children with this unique display. To prepare, tape the top and bottom of a photo of each child (facedown) to a different piece of construction paper. Cut an opening in the paper to reveal only the child's eyes in the photo. Then number each paper and make a list of the numbers and corresponding children for your reference. Display the covered photos during open house and invite parents to identify their children. When each parent tells you the correct number of the photo that shows his child, uncover the photo and give it to him to keep.

✳ These student-made gifts are a fun favor for parents to take home after their open house visit. To make a favor, a child cuts an apple shape from red craft foam. Next, she glues a green craft foam leaf and a brown craft foam stem to the apple. When the glue is dry, help her use a permanent marker to personalize her apple. Then attach a self-adhesive magnet strip to the back of the apple. Before open house, place each child's apple magnet on her desk for her parent(s) to find.

How do I **build a sense of classroom community**?

✱ Help students work together to make a classroom banner. Set out a large sheet of bulletin board paper. Then lead youngsters in discussing how they can decorate the banner. Once a consensus is reached, invite children to work together to decorate the banner. Hang the banner in a prominent location to remind students that they are a team.

Joshua MaKenna Pierce Sasha

Mrs. Robertson's Class

Emma Marisa Robby Vincent

✱ This catchy chant celebrates when a student helps a classmate. When a child lets you know that a friend helped him, lead youngsters in saying the chant to celebrate his good work. Then share with students what the youngster did to deserve the praise.

[Kevin, Kevin],
That's the way!
You helped [Ollie]
In a special way!

✱ Have youngsters brainstorm a list of school issues that bother them, such as having no one to play with at recess or not getting along with someone. Then divide students into groups and have each group come up with a possible solution for a different issue. Have the group discuss the issue and role-play a possible solution for the class.

How do I **arrange my room for learning**?

✳ To promote cooperation and teamwork, have students sit in groups. For each group, arrange four desks in a square. Then use a 12-inch bungee cord to bind together the four desk legs that meet in the center. Since the cord keeps the desks grouped, you won't need to straighten them at the end of the day.

✳ Define students' personal space with this circle-time idea. Put a class supply of inexpensive vinyl placemats on the floor in a desired seating arrangement. Have each child sit on a separate mat. There's no doubt youngsters will be better able to keep their hands and feet to themselves and focus their attention on you!

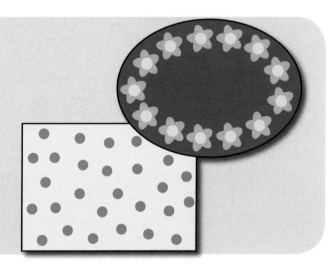

✳ Assign each classroom area a specific purpose. For example, designate areas for large-group activities, independent reading, and small-group work. The consistency helps youngsters remember the routines and expectations for the corresponding activities.

✳ Be sure each child's seat is positioned so he faces you during instruction. It's a surefire way to limit distractions and increase student accountability.

What **supplies should I have on hand**?

✱ It's ideal to have liquid glue as well as glue sticks. Some art projects require liquid glue for best results. Glue sticks, however, are better for cut-and-glue practice pages. They're a great less-mess option!

✱ Keep an assortment of writing tools in your classroom since young children experience success with different writing instruments. Different-size pencils, markers, crayons, and a selection of pencil-grip guides are great to have. The variety allows each youngster to try different options and discover what works best!

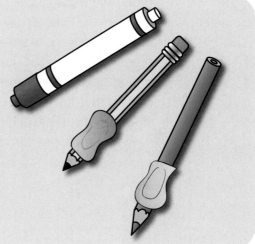

✱ Liquid watercolors are a must-have for any early childhood classroom. After all, they're not just for painting! Add a few drops of paint to a favorite play dough recipe. Dip a dried-out marker in paint to refresh it. A few drops of paint can revive a dried-out stamp pad too. Students will also love when you squirt a few drops of paint into non-mentholated shaving cream; it provides a colorful sensory experience!

How do I **cut down on classroom clutter**?

✱ Reduce classroom clutter by following this simple rule: When something comes in, something else must go out. Each time you introduce different materials or supplies, put away an item that's no longer needed.

✱ When classroom space is at a premium, rotating supplies keeps things tidy. Store items such as math manipulatives in labeled plastic shoeboxes. Periodically rotate the boxes from the classroom to a storage area. Since a limited number of materials are out at one time, the room is less crowded. As an added benefit, student interest stays high because new materials are introduced regularly.

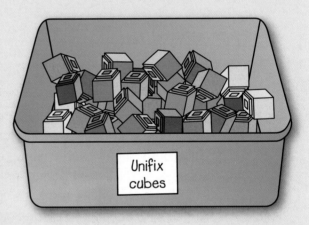

Unifix cubes

✱ Decrease clutter with a hanging shoe organizer. Hang the organizer in a closet or on the back of a door. The pockets are perfect for storing small items, such as manipulatives, letter and number cards, and art supplies.

How do I **decorate my classroom on a budget**?

✱ Check out dollar stores and the dollar bins at department stores. They have lots of great items that are perfect for classroom use. Bargains include nameplates for student desks and seasonal decorations. Discount stores also have storage bins and bathroom caddies that are wonderful organizers to keep at centers or students' tables.

✱ Instead of buying an alphabet display, showcase student-decorated letters. Invite students to paint a set of poster board alphabet letters. Then have youngsters decorate the letters with arts-and-crafts materials, such as pom-poms, feathers, tissue paper squares, and glitter. It saves money and results in a one-of-a-kind display!

✱ Gift wrap is a fun alternative to store-bought bulletin board borders. Look for great deals at discount stores and at clearance sales after holidays. Use a strip of old border as a pattern or just cut the gift wrap into strips. Either way, you'll have an eye-catching border that's a bargain!

How do I **maximize space in a small classroom**?

✱ Strategically place low bookcases to create work areas. Arrange two bookcases back-to-back in order to allow for storage on the shelves and to divide work areas. If only one bookcase is available, it's no problem. Use it to divide an area. Then cover the back of the bookcase with bulletin board paper and encourage students to write and draw on it. The result is visually appealing and functional!

✱ Large, lidded plastic bins are perfect alternatives to established center areas. Store activity materials in bins to keep them out of sight. When it's center time, set out the bins in various locations around the room. Once students remove the materials from the bins, they can snap the lids back in place and use them for work surfaces.

✱ Use pants hangers to store posters and big books. Clip two posters back-to-back on a hanger. Then hang the posters in a closet to keep them out of view. Clip individual big books to hangers and then hang them on the sides of an easel. The books and posters stay in good condition, and you can find what you need in a jiffy!

How do I **get a display up fast**?

✳ For a quick year-round display, back a bulletin board with flame-retardant fabric. Put the hook sides of Velcro adhesive strips where you want changeable parts of the display, such as the title and main character. Put the loop sides of Velcro adhesive strips on the backs of items you'd like to showcase; then attach the items to the board. When it's time to update the display, simply peel off the pieces that have Velcro fasteners and replace them with different pieces!

✳ Level your title with ease. Stretch a length of yarn across a bulletin board and lightly tape it to the edges of the board so the yarn ends are at the same height. Attach the title to the display, keeping the bottom of the title flush with the yarn. Then remove the yarn. No more crooked titles!

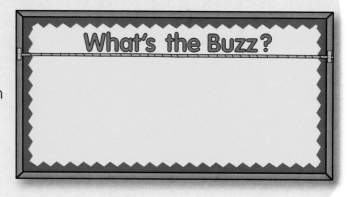

What's the Buzz?

✳ If you've run out of time to create a display, have students pitch in. Frame a bulletin board with double-sided tape. Have each child create a small piece of artwork. Then stick the artwork to the tape to create a one-of-a-kind border. Add a title such as "Creative Kids," and the display is complete.

How do I **manage cleanup with my students**?

✱ Use photos to make cleanup a snap. Take photos of toys, games, manipulatives, and other classroom items that have established storage places. Use clear packing tape to attach each photo to the appropriate storage shelf or container. When it's time to clean up, have students refer to the photos to ensure everything is returned to its proper place.

✱ Color-code classroom materials so young children can tidy the classroom independently. Assign a color to each area of the room, such as reading, math, discovery, manipulatives, and housekeeping. Attach sticky dots of a matching color to the materials in each area. Students can tell at a glance whether they're returning items to the correct areas.

✱ Motivate students to ready the classroom for the next day. Designate a few students to be the Clean Team. Present them with badges to wear while they tidy the classroom. There's no doubt the honored youngsters will be thrilled to get the room in tip-top condition!

The Clean Team

How do I **manage cleanup with my students**?

✳ Turn cleanup time into a game! Tell youngsters that you are thinking of a particular piece of trash on the floor but don't reveal which piece it is. Explain that you will give a prize to the youngster who throws away the secretly chosen piece of trash. Students are bound to pick up all the trash in nearly no time. After the room is clean, reveal which piece of trash is the secret one.

✳ Since puppets are fantastic motivational tools, why not designate a puppet to be the class cleanup mascot? During cleanup time, put the puppet on your hand and have it "watch" students tidy the room. Whenever the puppet observes a student doing a nice job, use the puppet to give the youngster a pat on the back.

✳ Encourage students to take ownership in how the classroom looks. Create a list of daily class jobs so each child has a duty. When you assign jobs, explain that each child will have the same job all year and he will be the class expert at it. Since each student has only one class job throughout the year, he's unlikely to forget his responsibility. In fact, he's sure to take pride in it!

How do I **manage arrival time**?

✳ Use a visual reminder to ensure that your students have the morning routine down pat. List on a piece of bulletin board paper the tasks you expect students to do upon arrival. Photograph a child engaged in each activity and post the corresponding photo next to each item. When students arrive in the morning, they complete each task on the list, using the photographs for assistance.

Morning Routine

1. Hang up your coat and backpack.

2. Sharpen your pencil.

3. Turn in notes from home.

✳ Help students transition into the school day at their own pace by offering them a choice of arrival activities. Familiarize students with a variety of centers and activities that can be completed independently. When each child arrives, invite him to participate in the center or activity of his choosing.

✳ Track students' attendance with this idea that doubles as a daily group-time activity. Near the classroom door, post a large simple schoolhouse cutout. For each student, attach a piece of the hook side of a Velcro fastener to the back of a trimmed photograph and the loop side of a piece of Velcro fastener to the schoolhouse. Place the photos in a container near the cutout. When each student arrives, she finds her photo and attaches it to the schoolhouse. During group time, count the number of present and absent students and compare the two numbers.

How do I **start each day on a positive note**?

✱ Set an upbeat tone in the classroom by playing lively music as students arrive. After students have organized their materials and gotten ready to start the day, invite them to dance to the music for a few minutes to release excess energy and get the wiggles out.

✱ Each day before students arrive, write a few encouraging words or a compliment on the board. When students have settled in, read the board aloud to help get the day started off right.

Today is going to be a great day! We will have fun and learn a lot.

✱ Get students excited about each day by highlighting a time or activity on your posted schedule. When the corresponding part of the day arrives, do something special prior to beginning the scheduled activity, such as singing a short song or allowing students a few minutes of free time.

✱ Welcome each student to the classroom and help give her a positive start to her day. Each morning, stand at the classroom door and offer each child a handshake, a hug, or a high five as she arrives. This simple gesture makes each child feel good while allowing her to choose how she would feel most comfortable being greeted.

How do I **help children with transitions**?

✱ To help youngsters move smoothly between activities, recite the chant shown. Then wait two minutes before moving on to the next task. This gentle warning helps little ones know it is time to finish the current activity and get ready to move on to something new.

Learn, laugh, work, and play.
We have lots to do today.
In two minutes, you will see
What our new activity will be.

✱ Teach students a few simple nonverbal cues to prompt transitions. When it is time to clean up and move on to the next activity, simply flash the lights or ring a bell. Teach students that these cues signal it is time to clean up and quietly go on to the next task.

✱ Use transition time for extra skill practice. Obtain a set of cards for practicing a desired skill, such as letter cards, color cards, or shape cards. When a student is ready to move on to the next task, show her a card. After she names the corresponding item, she can go on to the next activity.

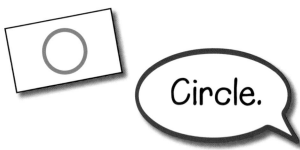

Circle.

✱ Transitioning from noisy or lively activities to calm, quiet ones can be a challenge. To help students, have them perform a simple breathing exercise. Have youngsters stand and lift their arms above their heads as they inhale and then move their arms back down to their sides as they exhale. After doing this several times, students should be calm enough to move on to the next task.

How do I **help young children line up**?

✳ To help students form a straight line, use clear packing tape to attach a class supply of die-cut shapes to the floor. Ensure that the shapes have adequate space between them. When it is time to line up, instruct each youngster to stand on a shape facing forward.

✳ Make your own walking rope using sturdy ribbon and shower curtain rings. Obtain a length of ribbon (one foot for each student) and a class supply of plastic shower curtain rings. Tie each ring onto the ribbon at one-foot intervals. When it is time to line up, have each child hold onto a ring before you lead the class to your destination.

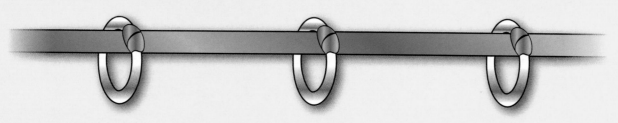

✳ This idea reminds students to keep their hands to themselves in line. After students are lined up, say, "Lock it or pocket!" Then have each youngster either clasp his hands in front of himself to "lock" them together or put his hands inside his pockets.

✳ Do your line leaders have trouble knowing where to begin the line? Attach a length of colored masking tape to the desired location on the floor a sufficient distance from your classroom door. When youngsters line up, the line leader places his toes just behind the tape to ensure he is starting the line in the proper spot.

How do I **promote good hallway behavior**?

✳ To keep students quiet in the hallway, encourage them to imagine that they are invisible. Tell youngsters not to make a sound and to walk very quietly so no one will know they are there.

✳ Instead of walking at the front or the back of your line, try walking in the middle. It enables you to keep a closer watch on all your students while walking from place to place.

✳ Encourage quiet passage through the hall with the help of a scavenger hunt. As youngsters line up, give clipboards (with pencils attached) to several students that exhibit especially good behavior. Next, announce items for students to look for as they walk through the hallway—such as letters, numbers, or shapes. Each student with a clipboard keeps track of what she finds as she walks. Invite the other students to keep a mental note of the items they discover. When you return to the classroom, invite youngsters to share their findings with the group. If desired, have colleagues help you by cleverly hiding predetermined items.

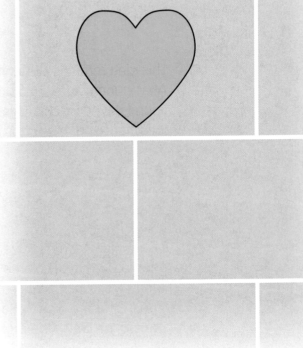

How do I **promote good hallway behavior**?

✳ Invite positive attention as your class walks through the hallway with this simple idea. Have students help you make a sign similar to the one shown. Invite your line leader to carry the sign as your class walks through the hallway. Each time someone compliments the class on their hallway behavior, attach a sticker to the sign. When a predetermined number of stickers have been earned, celebrate with extra recess time, a popcorn party, or another reward.

Please tell us how we are doing!

✳ This timely idea encourages youngsters to walk quietly in the hallway and keep their hands to themselves. Choose a seasonal item, such as a pumpkin or a snowflake. As students walk down the hallway, invite them to perform an action that corresponds to the chosen item, such as putting their arms in circles in front of them to make pumpkins or wiggling their fingers above their heads like falling snowflakes. Performing these actions keeps students engaged and reduces hallway chatter.

✳ This catchy chant motivates students to exhibit appropriate hallway behavior. After lining up, lead youngsters in saying, "Hand on my hip, and finger on my lip!" Then direct each child to put his left hand on his hip and the pointer finger of his right hand over his lips. Once each child is in this position, lead the class into the hallway. Not only will little ones be quiet, but their hands will be occupied as well.

How do I **manage bathroom and water breaks**?

✳ Cut down on interruptions from children requesting to go to the restroom by encouraging each child to simply raise two fingers (like a peace sign) to indicate her need. You can acknowledge each request with a simple nod of your head and continue teaching.

✳ To know at a glance who is in the restroom and who is taking a water break, label a sheet of paper as shown and laminate it. Post the sign near your classroom door. Then use a piece of Velcro fastener to attach a dry-erase marker to the sign. When a child needs a break, direct him to write his name (or his initials) in the appropriate column and wipe it clean when he is finished.

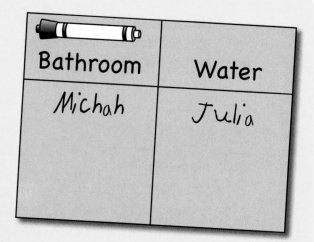

Bathroom	Water
Michah	Julia

✳ Do your youngsters often linger at the water fountain? Speed things along with a sand timer. Place a sand timer on the edge of the water fountain and instruct youngsters to turn it over just before they begin drinking. When all the sand has moved into the lower portion of the timer, that child's time is up and he must return to his seat.

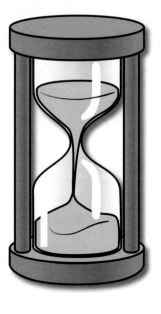

How do I **manage naptime**?

✳ Encourage your little ones to drift off to sleep with the help of a rest-time wand. To make one, cut two identical star shapes from tagboard. Brush one side of each star with glue and then sprinkle glitter on the stars. When the glue is dry, glue the stars together, glitter sides out, leaving an opening in the bottom. Hot-glue an unsharpened pencil in the opening. Wave the wand over each youngster's head at the beginning of rest time to help him fall asleep.

✳ A visit from the sticker fairy helps encourage quiet resting. In the middle of naptime, slip a crown of sparkly garland on your head to become the sticker fairy. Then gently place a sticker on the hand of each child who is sleeping or resting quietly.

✳ This idea promotes quiet resting, whether little ones are sleepy or not. At the beginning of rest time, invite each student to close her eyes and "create" a dream in her head. When rest time is over, invite a few volunteers to share the details of their dreams with the group.

✳ To keep youngsters who don't fall asleep during rest time occupied, post several nursery rhyme characters around the room. Encourage each student who is not tired to look at the characters and silently say the corresponding rhymes to himself.

How do I **manage snacktime**?

✳ Reinforce good manners while passing out snacks. Begin by asking each child whether he would like a serving of the snack. Have him respond by saying, "No, thank you" or "Yes, please." When children are comfortable answering that question, ask some giggle-inducing questions, such as "Would you like some purple pizza?" or "Would you like some frog leg stew?" It's a fun way to promote polite behavior!

✳ Organize snacktime with personalized placemats that double as student allergy reminders. Cut vinyl placemats in half vertically so there is one half per student. For each child, program an adhesive label with his name and any food allergies he has. Then attach the label to the placemat half.

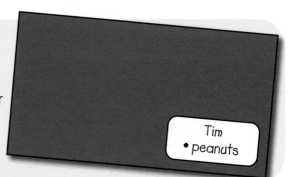

Tim
• peanuts

✳ Manage snacktime seating arrangements and teach name recognition at the same time. Use clear Con-Tact covering to attach a class supply of shape cutouts to a table. Assign seats by using erasable markers to write a different child's name on each shape. After snacktime, simply wipe the tables and shapes clean.

✳ Encourage parents to provide classroom snacks. Label each of five large, lidded buckets with a different day of the week and a snack request. Every Friday, send each bucket home with a different student. Have each family fill its bucket and return the bucket with the corresponding snack on Monday.

25 granola bars

How do I **manage outside time**?

✳ Prepare for outdoor incidents by making a handy first aid kit. In a plastic bucket place supplies such as adhesive bandages, moistened wipes, tissues, and cotton balls. Take the bucket with you each time you take the class outdoors to ensure that you're prepared to handle youngsters' minor injuries.

✳ Make the outdoors an extension of your classroom by setting up learning centers on the playground. A sensory center, gross-motor center, fine-motor center, water table, and sand table are kid-pleasing options. Invite students to rotate through the centers as they complete the activities. What a great way to jazz up center time when the weather gets warmer!

✳ Take only half the class with you when you venture outside. Leave the other half of the class inside with another staff member. A smaller group is easier to supervise, and students are more likely to remain on task.

✳ Store outdoor play equipment in a rolling laundry hamper. It is large enough to hold your supplies and light enough that a student can help roll it outside.

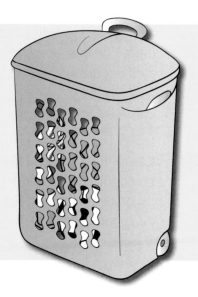

How do I celebrate student birthdays?

✳ At the beginning of the year, invite each child to decorate a cupcake cutout. Then have her glue candle cutouts on the cupcake to match her age. Post a number cutout for each age represented in your class and attach each cupcake below the corresponding number. On a child's birthday, have her glue an additional candle cutout to her cupcake; then display the cupcake under her new age.

✳ Honor a birthday child with a special serenade. Gather students in a circle around the child and have them hold hands. Direct them to walk in a circle around the youngster as they sing a birthday song. (If the song has more than one verse, guide students to change the direction they are walking for each verse.) Then lead students in cheering, "Hip, hip, hooray!" as they raise their hands and walk toward the center of the circle. Repeat the cheer a number of times equal to the birthday child's age.

✳ Instead of celebrating multiple birthdays each month, choose one day to recognize all the students born in that month. Coordinate snacks and other celebration details with the families of the birthday boys and girls to make the day memorable.

How do I **celebrate student birthdays**?

✱ On the day of a youngster's birthday celebration, attach festive wrapping paper, ribbons, and bows to his desk or cubby. No doubt he will feel special when he sees this colorful presentation.

✱ Showcase students' birthdates with a month-by-month display. Choose a different seasonal cutout for each month. Attach each child's picture to a cutout that corresponds with her birth month and label it with her name and birthdate. Display the cutouts according to month. At the beginning of each month, move the appropriate monthly cutouts to a featured location by the calendar.

✱ Present each youngster with a student-made birthday book. To make one, have students brainstorm words that describe the birthday child as you list them on the board. Then direct each student to draw a picture of the honored youngster and write (or dictate for you to write) a descriptive caption below it. Bind the completed pages between two construction paper covers. This book will be a much-treasured gift!

Nick is kind to others.

How do I **welcome a new student**?

✳ Help a transfer student make a friend in your class. On the first day, pair him with another student. Encourage the two to come up with something they have in common by the end of the day. The challenge helps the students get acquainted quickly and sparks an instant connection.

✳ Use this booklet to help new students learn their classmates' names. For each student currently in your class, glue a photo to a separate piece of paper. Have each child personalize his page; then bind the pages between two construction paper covers. Present the booklet to a transfer student on her first day in your classroom.

✳ Assist a new student in learning about his new classroom and his classmates' names. Gather the class in a circle and introduce the new student. Have each child, in turn, share her name and what she likes best about the classroom. Then invite the new student to ask any questions he has about the room.

My name is Sarah. I like the block center!

How do I **welcome a non-English-speaking child**?

✳ Use an ELL (English Language Learner) student's name to welcome her to your classroom. Write the letters in the student's name vertically on the board. Then invite the class to brainstorm descriptive words about the new student. Have the class help the ELL student choose one adjective or phrase per letter as you write it on the board. Share the completed acrostic poem with the class.

Many friends
Always kind
Rarely mad
Interesting
Speaks Spanish
Outgoing
Laughs a lot

✳ A picture dictionary offers an ELL student a great way to practice vocabulary. Ask students to help you cut a variety of pictures from magazines. Glue the pictures on separate pages in a blank book and then label them. The student can flip through the book at school or take it home for extra practice.

apple

✳ Assign each ELL student a buddy that he can shadow. After partnering the new student with a child from the class, instruct him to follow the student and mimic his actions. Have the buddy help the ELL child as needed, and make sure he is in the right places at the proper times. This will help the ELL student learn the routine as he gradually overcomes the language barrier.

How does my class **say goodbye to a student who is leaving**?

❋ Invite youngsters to share positive messages with a child who is leaving your class. Have each child draw a picture of the student and then write or dictate something special about that student. On the child's last day in class, invite her to sit in a place of honor as each student reads his message and presents her with the paper as a keepsake.

Zoe always shared her snacks with me.

❋ Give the child a disposable camera and a supply of stamped school-addressed envelopes. Invite him to take photographs of his new home, neighborhood, and school. Then encourage him to mail the pictures to your class with a letter telling about the photos. If desired, have your students write back to the child, telling him what they liked about his photos and asking any questions they have.

❋ Give the child a memento of the friendships he has in your class. Take a photo of the departing child with each of his classmates. Attach each photo to a separate sheet of paper. Then invite each student to write (or dictate for you to write) a special memory about the child. Bind the completed pages in a book between two construction paper covers.

How do I **manage dismissal time**?

✳ Motivate youngsters to get packed up in a hurry! On separate slips of paper write rhymes, songs, or cheers that are popular with your students. Fold the papers and place them in a box. If time permits after students have packed up their belongings, invite a child to take a paper from the box and then lead the group in the corresponding activity.

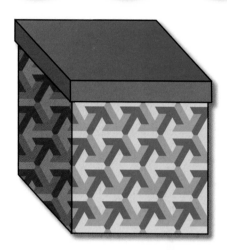

✳ Keep students quietly watching you as they wait to line up. Have youngsters sit on the floor and look at you. Intently fix your gaze on one student at a time, indicating it is her turn to line up.

✳ Promote home-school connections while keeping dismissal time running smoothly. Place a table by your classroom door. Throughout the day, place on the table books, projects, and other items that represent the day's activities. As children are getting ready to leave, encourage them to look at the table to review the day's events. Since the day is sure to stay fresh in their minds, they're bound to share the information with their families!

✳ Write the names of simple games on separate cards. Hole-punch the cards and attach them to a metal ring. If your students are ready for dismissal early, flip to a card and lead them in the game while they wait.

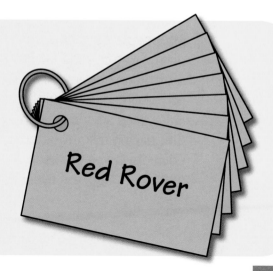

Red Rover

How do I **stay on top of paperwork**?

✱ Use tabbed dividers to divide a large binder into sections such as schedule, lesson plans, parent communication, conference notes, staff meeting notes, and other useful information. Then place the corresponding paperwork in each section. Important paperwork stays together so you can easily refer to it when needed.

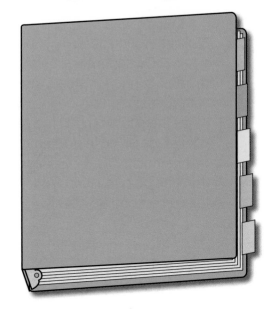

✱ Delegate some paperwork tasks to parent volunteers. Ask for volunteers to assume tasks such as coordinating book orders or creating and distributing flyers about upcoming classroom events. This is a great way for parents to help out in your classroom, plus it saves you valuable time.

✱ Designate a block of time each day for doing paperwork. Set a timer for a desired amount of time and spend that time doing tasks such as grading papers, answering parent notes, or completing other school paperwork. When the timer goes off, move on to a different activity. Completing a small amount of paperwork each day helps you keep on top of it while also making it seem less overwhelming.

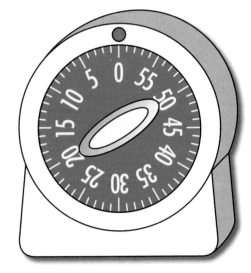

How do I **organize student papers**?

✳ A plastic crate is perfect for organizing students' work papers. Personalize a hanging folder for each child; then store the folders in alphabetical order in the crate. After you check a child's paper, slip it in his file. When it is time to send a student's work home, simply remove his papers from the hanging file and place them in his take-home folder.

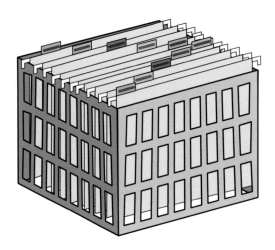

✳ Keep students' finished and unfinished work organized with colored trays. Set out red and green trays. When work time is over, a child places completed projects in the red tray. She places projects that she still needs to finish in the green tray.

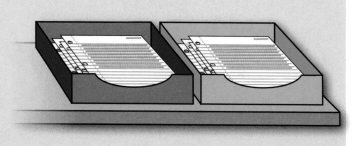

✳ This simple checklist helps you keep track of who has turned in assignments and who has not. Make a copy of a class list. As each student turns in an assignment, make a check mark beside her name. Clip the completed assignment behind the copy of the list. You'll know at a glance who still owes you that assignment.

How do I **organize and maintain a classroom library**?

✳ Students can quickly find books of interest when your classroom library is organized by genre. Assign each genre a different color; then attach a corresponding colored sticky dot to each book. Shelve the books by color so youngsters can easily find the type of book they are looking for.

✳ Try sorting your books by favorite characters or themes. Place books for each character or theme in a tub along with toys that are related to the books. Invite youngsters to read the books to the toys or to hold the toys while they read.

✳ Keep your classroom library fresh by organizing your books by the months of the year. Sort books in separate lidded containers according to the appropriate month. Include books that relate to holidays and themes that you will teach during that month. At the beginning of each month, change the books in your classroom library by replacing them with the contents of the appropriate box.

How do I **make the most of my planning period**?

✱ At the beginning of the school year, use a computer program to make a template of your planbook pages. Fill in the information that stays the same each week, such as lunch and recess times. Staple a printout of the template to each week's plan book pages. You won't waste precious time writing the same information each week, and you can devote more time to planning cool learning experiences!

✱ Use monthly outlines to make short work of weekly planning. At the beginning of each month, jot down skills, topics, themes, and other key planning information on a monthly graphic organizer like the one shown. When it's time to write more specific weekly plans, you'll have a head start!

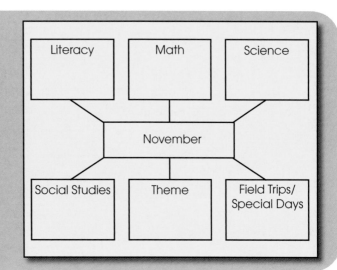

✱ Since a variety of tasks often vie for your attention during planning periods, make planning your first priority. Use the first half of the period to work on your lesson plans and the second half to check your mailbox, touch base with colleagues, or complete other tasks on your to-do list. That way, miscellaneous tasks won't rob you of all your planning time!

How do I **plan for multiple ages and skill levels**?

✳ Use your learning center time to work with small groups. Keep a list of students with similar skill needs for easy reference. When students are at centers, take that time to individualize instruction with small groups. It's a wonderful opportunity to jot assessment notes too!

✳ Open-ended activities and multiuse manipulatives are perfect for a range of skill needs. They allow for children to work at their own levels. For example, when students visit a learning center with letter manipulatives, they can practice a variety of skills, such as alphabetical order, forming spelling words, or creating word families. Every student can experience success!

✳ Incorporate a theme into your lesson planning. It's an excellent way to tie together differentiated activities. Since every student works on the same topic, it saves planning time and promotes a strong classroom community.

How do I **promote kindness and respect**?

✻ Boost student's self-esteem while promoting kindness. Sit with youngsters in a circle and have a volunteer sit in the center of the circle. Invite students to share something nice about the child in the center. Then ask a different volunteer to sit in the center of the circle. Continue until each child has sat in the center of the circle.

✻ Encourage students to recognize their own positive behaviors. Near the end of the school day, invite each student to share something positive he did, such as helping clean up, sharing toys, using kind words, or showing respect. Then praise his efforts and have him attach a star sticker to a class star cutout. After the cutout is filled with stickers, reward the class with a special treat or privilege.

✻ Invite youngsters to watch their kind deeds add up. To prepare, make a predetermined number of heart cutouts. When a child exhibits especially kind behavior, write his deed on a personalized heart and attach it to a display. When each heart has been added to the display, reward youngsters with a popcorn party or extra recess time.

I helped Kali
tie her shoes.

–Dylan

How do I **help students become responsible**?

✳ Encourage students to become responsible for keeping the classroom clean and orderly. After a messy activity, whenever the floor needs tidying, ask each child to pick up a piece of paper from the floor. Explain that each piece is a ticket and that each child will need a ticket to join the group's next activity. When paper scraps are at their worst, request two or more tickets from each student.

✳ A responsibility contest helps maintain good discipline. Divide the class into groups. Award groups responsibility points for demonstrating good conduct, kindness toward others, good sportsmanship, and class participation. Honor the winning group by giving its members ten minutes of free time or another special treat.

✳ Encourage students to turn in important paperwork with this incentive. Each morning, instruct students to place any paperwork (such as homework papers, parent notes, or permission slips) in a designated location. From time to time, check students' backpacks for important papers. Slip a small treat into each backpack belonging to a child who has turned in her important paperwork.

How do I **deal with talkativeness at inappropriate times**?

✳ When youngsters need a reminder about excess chatter, call out, "Marshmallow mouths!" Then direct each child to pretend to put a marshmallow in her mouth. This helps keep students' mouths occupied and cuts down on talking.

✳ Get noisy students' attention in a positive way. When student chatter is getting out of hand, begin counting slowly. As each child notices you counting, he joins in. When all (or most) of the class is counting with you, stop and write the last number you said on the board. Encourage youngsters to work toward having that number close to one the next time you begin counting due to the noise level.

1, 2, 3, 4, 5, 6...

✳ During group work, place a stuffed toy in the middle of each group. If a group gets too noisy, remove its toy. At the end of work time, praise each group that still has a stuffed toy.

✳ Use simple commands to quiet talkative students. When children get too chatty, give commands, such as, "Put your hands on your hips" and "Raise your hand." As youngsters hear you, they perform the corresponding action. Continue giving commands until you have each child's attention.

How do I **handle tattling**?

✱ Give youngsters guidelines to help determine when something should be shared with you, or if it is tattling. Ask a student to consider if the behavior in question hurts him or someone else, or if it breaks a classroom or school rule. If it does either of these things, encourage him to tell you immediately. If it does not, direct him to keep the information to himself.

✱ Decorate a small lidded box and label it as shown. Then cut a slit in the lid. Place paper and crayons nearby. If a student wants to tell you something about another student, have him draw a picture of it or write about it on a piece of paper labeled with his name. Then ask him to drop it in the box. Periodically check the box. As you look over the papers, decide which ones you need to handle and which ones can be discarded. Students are often satisfied because they "told" someone about the issue.

Tattling Box

✱ Instead of tattling to you, have students tell Tillie. Post a large picture of an elephant within student reach. Tell youngsters that the elephant's name is Tillie and that she is a great listener because of her big ears. When a child has something to tell, invite her to go to the poster and whisper what she needs to share in Tillie's ear.

Tell It to Tillie!

How do I **handle tattling**?

✳ Place a toy telephone in your classroom and call it the Tattle Phone. When a student wants to tattle, have him talk about it on the Tattle Phone. Secretly listen to the conversation to see if the child needs assistance with a more serious issue.

✳ Sometimes classmates can help students distinguish between tattling and sharing important news. Invite a child to share her information with a buddy from the class. Have the buddy help her determine if the situation needs teacher involvement. If it does, the pair reports it to the teacher right away. If it does not, the pair keeps it to themselves.

✳ Invite students to share their tattles with Tattle Tiger. Place a stuffed tiger in an easy-to-reach location. When a youngster feels the need to tattle, have him first share his tattle with the tiger. After doing this, if he still feels it is something he must share with you, encourage him to do so.

How do I **reach an unmotivated student**?

✳ Give students choices about their assignments. Allow students to choose the order in which they complete their assignments or have them select problems they want to complete from a list of options. Having choices about their work helps youngsters feel more in control, and they are more likely to begin working right away.

✳ Make copies of this poem to motivate youngsters to do their best. When a student seems unmotivated, tape a copy to his desk as a reminder of what he should do each day.

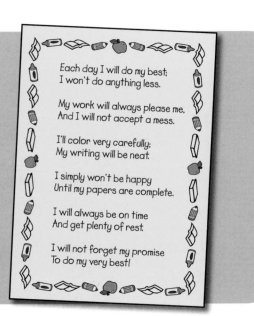

Each day I will do my best;
I won't do anything less.

My work will always please me,
And I will not accept a mess.

I'll color very carefully;
My writing will be neat.

I simply won't be happy
Until my papers are complete.

I will always be on time
And get plenty of rest.

I will not forget my promise
To do my very best!

✳ Observe unmotivated students over a few days and note times they show enthusiasm. If a child works best in a small group, arrange for her to work in a group as often as possible. Or, if she does better working independently, plan for her to work on her own when you can. Small changes such as these can make a big difference when it comes to student motivation!

How do I **help a child separate from a caregiver**?

✳ Ask a caregiver to spend time helping his child settle into an activity before he leaves the room. Since children love to interact with their environment, involving a child in a play activity with her caregiver will help her transition more easily.

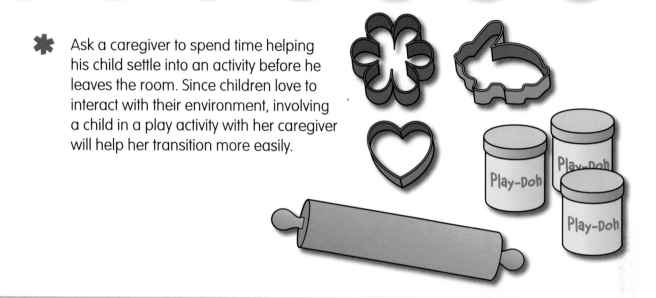

✳ Encourage the caregiver to establish a departure ritual to be repeated daily. She could read a book with her child, let her child hold a family photo or a familiar item when she leaves, or wave goodbye to him from the window. Repeating the same procedure each day helps a youngster become familiar with the routine and know when it is time to expect his caregiver to leave.

✳ Sometimes it is easier for a child to separate from her caregiver outside the classroom. If this is the case, meet each child at the door as she arrives. Have her say goodbye to her caregiver outside the classroom as you greet the student and welcome her inside.

How do I **help children work through disagreements**?

✱ To teach youngsters to take turns when they discuss a misunderstanding, decorate a cardboard tube and designate it the Talking Stick. Explain to students that the person holding the stick is the only one allowed to speak. When youngsters have a disagreement, instruct them to pass the stick back and forth, taking turns talking, until they have worked out their problem.

✱ Use a simple chant to help students calm themselves before confronting another student. When a youngster is upset, direct him to say to himself, "Stop. Count. In and out." Have him stop what he is doing, count to ten, and then take a deep breath in and out. It's sure to set the stage for a peaceful resolution!

✱ Provide a place for students to practice conflict resolution. Establish an area in your classroom called the Friendship Corner. When youngsters are involved in a dispute, invite them to go to the designated area to talk about their problem. Often, removing students from the problematic situation is enough to diffuse it.

How do I **work with a child who blurts out**?

✱ Provide positive reinforcement to students who don't blurt out, and those who do are sure to change their ways! When children raise their hands to speak, use a rubber stamp and an ink pad to stamp each child's hand. This provides a great incentive for students to raise their hands when they have something to say.

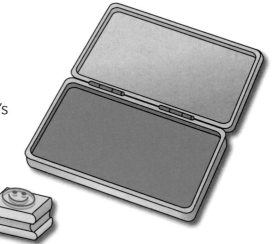

✱ Sometimes a child who blurts out does so because he is afraid he will forget what he wants to say. To address this concern, encourage him to draw a picture or write what he wants to say on a sheet of paper. Then have him raise his hand and wait for his turn to speak.

✱ A visual reminder helps cut down on interruptions from students who call out. Post near the front of the room a picture of a child raising her hand. When a child blurts out, point to the picture to remind him of what he is supposed to do to let you know he has something to say.

How do I **help a shy child**?

✱ Placing a shy child in a leadership role is sure to boost his participation and self-confidence. Designate the student as the "student teacher" and invite him to help with tasks such as leading chants, passing out papers and supplies, and running errands. Being involved in classroom activities such as these can bring a shy child out of his shell.

✱ Support shy students in your classroom with the help of puppets. Wear a puppet on your hand and use it to interact with youngsters. Have the puppet ask students questions, share information, and respond to students' questions. Not only will shy students feel more comfortable dealing with a puppet, but other students will enjoy it as well!

✱ During free play time or center time, sit near the shy child and start a conversation with nearby students. Ask the reluctant child questions to involve her in the conversation. Once the child is talking more easily, gradually move away.

How do I **deal with a child who bites**?

✱ Use a small stuffed animal to reinforce the importance of not biting others. Tell youngsters that the animal's name is Nippy and that he bites. Explain that you need students' help to remind Nippy not to bite others. Have students take turns being in charge of Nippy for a short time, beginning with the child who bites. Invite that child to care for Nippy as often as needed and encourage him to praise Nippy for his good behavior.

✱ Keep track of a youngster's biting behavior to see whether there is a pattern. Record each biting incident on a calendar, including who the child bit and what time of day the incident happened. The documentation can help you determine whether there is a way to change the child's behavior by modifying her routine. For example, if she always bites the same child, separate the two. Or if she always bites at the same time of day, it may be because she is hungry.

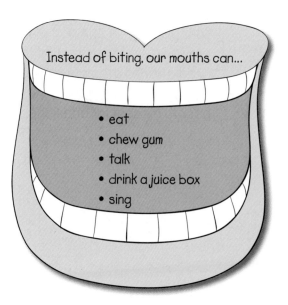

Instead of biting, our mouths can...

• eat
• chew gum
• talk
• drink a juice box
• sing

✱ Have students help you brainstorm things they can do instead of biting. Record their ideas on a poster like the one shown. Display the completed poster. When a child is tempted to bite, direct his attention to the poster to remind him of appropriate ways to use his mouth.

How do I **calm an upset child**?

✱ Prepare a "smile box" to have on hand when an upset child needs time to settle down. Place in a decorated box items such as a stress ball, a container of silly putty, and small puzzles. When a child is having trouble calming down, invite her to choose a "smile" item from the box. Then lead her to a quiet corner of the room where she can play with the item until she calms down.

✱ Soothe an upset youngster by asking her unexpected questions. Ask questions such as, "What color is your bedroom?" or "Which do you prefer, hot dogs or pizza?" She may be caught off guard by the questions and calm down to answer you. Once she is calm, you can more easily address whatever upset her.

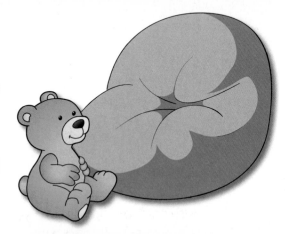

✱ To provide a special area in which an upset student can settle down, put comfortable seating—such as a bean bag chair or large floor pillows—in one part of the room. Also provide a stuffed animal for the child to cuddle. When the child is ready to rejoin the group, allow him to bring the stuffed animal back to his seat for additional comfort.

✱ A soft blanket can relax a distressed youngster. When a child is upset, invite him to wrap up in the blanket until he calms down.

How do I **deal with inappropriate language**?

✱ Let students know that if they are unsure whether something is appropriate to say, they can ask you for guidance. Have students ask you privately about the appropriateness of a word instead of disturbing the class by verbalizing the undesired word.

✱ When you hear a child use inappropriate words or phrases, tell her they are not "school words." Let her know there are certain words and phrases that should not be used at school and that the words she said are among them. Then suggest an alternative word or phrase to use that is appropriate for school.

✱ Some youngsters use inappropriate language as a way of expressing their emotions. Discuss with students different emotions such as anger, sadness, and frustration. As a class, brainstorm appropriate ways to respond to these emotions. Then have each child draw a picture of an appropriate way to deal with her emotions. Bind students' pictures between two construction paper covers. Display the book for children to look at when then are experiencing a troubling emotion.

How do I **manage a defiant child**?

✱ Ask a child who frequently disrupts class to be your assistant. Have her sit or stand beside you as you teach and help you gather and pass out materials. This alleviates constant interruptions. Plus, handling the behavior in a positive way can have a positive effect on the student's self-esteem, which may, in turn, improve her behavior.

✱ Give an aggressive student a goal to work toward. Write a behavior goal on a sticky note and attach the note to the corner of the child's desk or workspace. Each day that the youngster meets his goal, attach a sticker to his note. When a child collects a predetermined number of stickers, give him a small reward and have him take the sticky note home to show his family.

I will sit quietly
at circle time.

✱ Assign each youngster a cool-down spot in the classroom. If a child becomes disruptive, have her move to her cool-down spot for a break. Encourage her to perform relaxing actions such as taking a deep breath or doing arm stretches. Have her continue until she calms down and is ready to rejoin the group.

How do I **help a perfectionist child**?

✱ Encourage a perfectionist child to take breaks as he works so he will not become stressed. Allow him to stop working as needed to perform simple stretching exercises, practice deep breathing, or listen to a few minutes of soothing music. He's sure to relax and resume the task with less anxiety.

✱ Help a perfectionist student realize the benefits of making mistakes. Explain to the child that it is important to make mistakes because people learn from them. Tell about a mistake that you made and describe what you learned from it. Over time, the child may be willing to discuss mistakes he made and what he can learn from them.

✱ Remind students that mistakes are not a sign of failure but are proof of learning and growing. Tell students to think of mistakes as being like spices in foods: they are good in moderation. Label a clean and empty plastic spice bottle as shown. Before beginning an assignment or assessment, encourage the perfectionist child to "sprinkle" the contents of the bottle over his paper to remind himself that there is nothing wrong with making a few mistakes.

Mistake Jar

How do I **help a special needs child**?

✳ If a child has difficulty sitting still during circle time or other learning situations, invite him to hold an object such as a seashell, stress ball, or special rock. Holding the object keeps the child's hands busy so he can focus his attention on the current task.

✳ Use this idea to help students who have trouble transitioning to different activities. Set out a box labeled as shown. When a child is working on an assignment, give him ample warning about when it should be turned in. At the appropriate time, have him place his completed work in the box. He's less likely to engage in repetitive behaviors and can move on to the next activity more easily.

✳ Using scissors is a challenge for many students with special needs. To assist them in cutting out small pictures, use a broad marker to draw a loose outline around each picture. Have the child cut along the marker lines instead of attempting to cut out the pictures.

✳ To make transitions easier for special needs students, draw separate pictures to signify each of the day's activities. At the start of the day, post the first activity's picture on the board. When it is almost time to switch to the next activity, post the appropriate picture beside the first one to indicate the impending transition. Remove the first picture when students start the second activity. Continue in this manner throughout the day to help youngsters prepare for transitions.

How do I **help children develop patience**?

✳ Teach students the chant shown. Encourage each student to recite the chant whenever he needs to wait for his turn.

> Waiting is so hard to do.
> I need patience to get through.
> This is something I must learn:
> To wait until it is my turn.

✳ Provide a timer for a child who struggles with patience. Set the timer at the beginning of the activity to show how long it will be until the next activity. This visual tool helps the child know how much longer she has to wait and will eliminate interruptions.

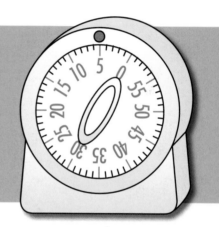

✳ Teach numeration as you promote patience. To help children wait for your individual attention, label five index cards, each with a different number from one to five. Put the cards in order; then store them in a student accessible location. When a child needs your help, have him take a number. Announce numbers to indicate whose turn it is to have your attention.

✳ Have students brainstorm a list of things they can do whenever they need to wait. The list could include activities such as practicing counting, quietly talking to a neighbor, or playing I Spy or another quiet game. Whenever students need to wait, they will already know what they can do to keep themselves occupied.

How do I **help children learn to share**?

✱ Use pom-poms for colorful reminders to share. Simply place a supply of pom-poms in a bowl near a transparent container labeled as shown. When you see a child sharing, invite her to place a pom-pom in the container. When the container is full of pom-poms, reward the class with a special snack or privilege.

Sharing Jar

✱ Lead youngsters in singing this song to help them learn about sharing. After singing, have youngsters help you brainstorm a list of things they can share with others.

(sung to the tune of "If You're Happy and You Know It")

If you're snacking on an apple, share a slice.
If you're snacking on an apple, share a slice.
Share a slice because it's nice.
When you share, you show you care.
If you're snacking on an apple, share a slice.

If you're playing with a toy, take your turn.
If you're playing with a toy, take your turn.
Take your turn, and you will learn.
When you share, you show you care.
If you're playing with a toy, take your turn.

If you're looking at a book, show a friend.
If you're looking at a book, show a friend.
Show a friend to start a trend.
When you share, you show you care.
If you're looking at a book, show a friend.

✱ Invite your class to practice sharing together. Designate a toy stuffed bear as Sharing Bear. Explain that the bear is a friend for the whole class to share. Have students take turns being in charge of Sharing Bear.

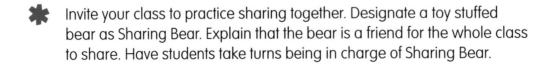

How do I **promote self-esteem**?

✳ Encourage youngsters to celebrate their uniqueness with this little ditty. Lead youngsters in singing the song. Then have each child, in turn, name something that makes him special.

> *(sung to the tune of "Take Me Out to the Ballgame")*
>
> I am unique and special.
> There is only one me!
> Nobody else walks the way I walk;
> Nobody else talks the way that I talk.
> And I'm very glad that I'm special;
> I am glad that I'm me!
> There is no one else in the world
> I would rather be!

✳ Pair a student with low self-esteem with a younger child or a child who is struggling. Have the first child listen to his buddy read, provide tutoring, or give other special help. He'll gain confidence in his abilities, and the other child will benefit from the extra assistance. It's a win-win situation!

✳ Give students' self-esteem a boost by helping them realize all the things they can do. Take photos of youngsters engaged in activities, making sure to take at least one photo of each child. Invite each child to glue a photo of himself to a sheet of paper and then dictate a caption for you to write. Bind the completed pages into a class book. When a youngster needs a self-esteem boost, invite him to read the book and see what he can do!

I can tie my shoes!

How do I **reward good or improved behavior**?

✱ Good behavior deserves a high five! Keep a supply of hand-shaped cutouts in an accessible location. When you see a youngster exhibiting exceptional or improved behavior, write her name and the behavior on a cutout and present it to the child as you give her a high five. Count on students to be eager to take their hand cutouts home to share with their families!

Cayleigh walked in the hall!

✱ Put youngsters' good behavior on display. When you spot a student showing good behavior, snap a photograph of her. Label the photo with a caption identifying the praiseworthy behavior. Display the photos and the captions in the room to remind youngsters of their good behaviors.

✱ Celebrate students' improved behavior with a paper chain. Cut a supply of colorful paper strips. Each time your students achieve a predetermined behavior goal, make a loop with a paper strip. Connect the loops to make a chain. When the chain reaches a certain number of links, reward the class with extra playtime or a special snack.

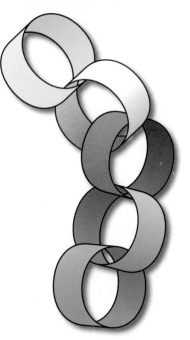

How do I **reward good or improved behavior**?

✻ Cut brightly colored paper into different-shaped blobs. When a child shows exceptional behavior, write his deed on a cutout. Showcase the cutouts with the title "Bright Spots in Our Classroom."

Ian was a good friend to Say'Quan.

✻ Make a supply of fake money (behavior bucks) and stock a classroom store with inexpensive items. Each time a child exhibits good or improved behavior, give him a behavior buck. At the end of the week, invite students to use their behavior bucks to shop in your classroom store.

Behavior Buck

✻ Designate a classroom window as the Window of Fame. When you notice a child exhibiting especially good behavior, invite him to use a window marker to write his name on the window. Students are thrilled to write on the windows, and the names of youngsters with good behavior are displayed for many people to see.

How do I **keep parents informed**?

✱ Prior to the beginning of the year, prepare a packet of information that includes general school information, classroom procedures, your discipline plan, and ways to help a child at home. Encourage parents to keep this packet handy so they can refer to it throughout the year.

✱ A classroom website is a great way to keep parents up to date. Each week, add to the website information such as upcoming events, reminders, homework assignments, and classroom photos. Send an email to parents to let them know when new information has been added to the site.

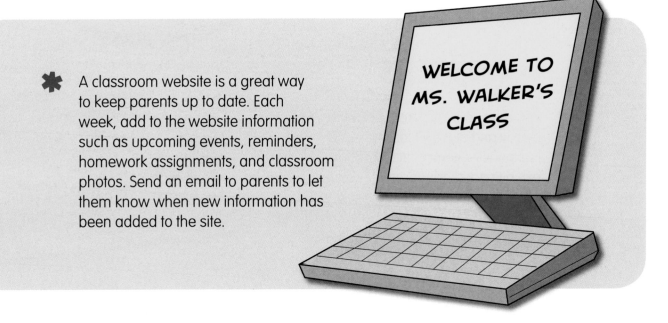

WELCOME TO MS. WALKER'S CLASS

✱ Keep parents in the know about your classroom with this display. Near the door, set up a display titled "Parent Corner." Include details about upcoming events, needed classroom supplies, and extra copies of notes that were recently sent home. Parents can refer to this display as needed.

How do I **keep parents informed**?

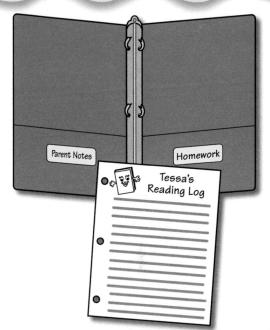

❋ At the beginning of the school year, ask each parent to send in a three-ring binder. Label the binder pockets as shown. At the beginning of each month, hole-punch a personalized reading log for each child and place it in her binder. Each day, slip notes from you or the school, the child's homework sheet, and other homework-related papers in the appropriate pockets. Have parents check the binder each evening and then place papers in the appropriate place(s). Each morning, remove any notes or homework papers from each child's binder.

❋ Encourage children to share details about special school events with their families. After a special school event or field trip, make a class set of labels like the ones shown. (Use a word processing program to quickly make the labels.) Attach a label to each child's shirt prior to dismissal.

> Ask me who visited my school.

> Ask me about the trip to the fire station.

❋ Share with parents the weekly happenings in your classroom with a class-made story. Each afternoon, invite students to help you write a short story about what happened at school that day. At the end of the week, combine the daily stories and send a copy home to each family. Families will appreciate reading about their child's week from the students' perspectives.

How do I **communicate with parents on the phone**?

✱ Open up the lines of communication by making a point to call each child's family sometime during the first month of school. Share something encouraging about their child and invite the family to share information about the child that may be helpful. You can also use this time to answer any questions that the family may have.

✱ Throughout the year, take the time to make upbeat calls to parents. Each week, choose two students and call their families to share something positive about their children. It doesn't take much time, and parents really appreciate this simple gesture.

✱ Keep a record of telephone calls to and from parents. Personalize a phone log, similar to the one shown, for each child. Store the logs in a three-ring binder. Each time you communicate with a family over the phone, record it on the appropriate log and jot down a brief note about the conversation. If the need arises, you can refer to the log to refresh your memory about a particular conversation.

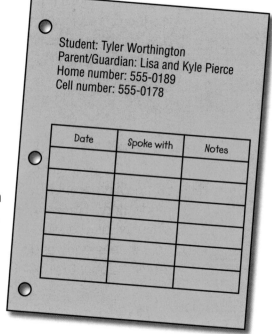

Student: Tyler Worthington
Parent/Guardian: Lisa and Kyle Pierce
Home number: 555-0189
Cell number: 555-0178

Date	Spoke with	Notes

How do I **communicate with parents in written form**?

✳ Give parents the opportunity to ask questions without interrupting class time. Decorate a lidded box similar to the one shown. Then cut a slit in the lid of the box. Set the box out along with paper slips and pens. When a parent has a question that does not need an immediate answer, have her write it on a paper slip and drop it in the box. Prior to writing your next class newsletter, read the questions in the box. Then publish the questions and their answers in your newsletter.

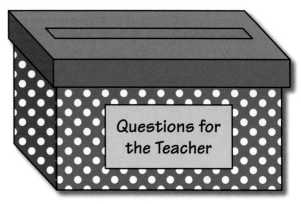

Questions for the Teacher

✳ Here's a simple way to keep a record of written communication with parents. Personalize a spiral-bound notebook for each child and store each student's notebook in his bookbag. Encourage parents to write notes to you in the notebook. Write your responses and other notes to parents in the notebook as well. If necessary, you can refer to the previous notes in the notebook to help keep track of your communications.

✳ Capture youngsters' achievements and triumphs in a spiral-bound notebook. Write each child's name at the top of a separate page. When a child accomplishes something, write a quick note and the date on her page. At the end of the school year, type each child's list and print it on decorative paper for parents.

How do I **hold a successful conference**?

✳ Personalize a folder for each child. Inside each folder place a copy of the child's report card, work samples, and other items you would like to share with a parent. When it is time for a conference, have the child's folder ready. The necessary paperwork will be at your fingertips so you can easily answer each parent's questions and address areas of growth and concern.

✳ Planning ahead ensures that you can successfully address parent concerns during a conference. Prior to a conference, send the parents a questionnaire similar to the one shown. Ask the parents to complete the questionnaire and return it to you before the conference. Use the information to help you prepare.

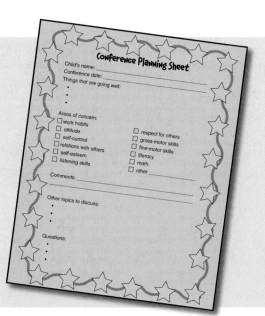

✳ Use conferences to help ease parents' anxiety about assessments. Set out manipulatives and other items that are used to assess students. Demonstrate assessments so parents have an idea of how their child is assessed. You can also encourage parents to use some of the demonstrated methods when working with their child at home.